The Horse Fair

Pitt Poetry Series

Ed Ochester, Editor

Robin Becker

The Horse Fair

POEMS

University of Pittsburgh Press

The publication of this book is supported by grants from
the Pennsylvania Council on the Arts and
the National Endowment for the Arts

Published by the University of Pittsburgh Press, Pittsburgh, Pa., 15261

Manufactured in the United States of America

Printed on acid-free paper

10 9 8 7 6 5 4 3 2 1

Title page drawing: Rosa Bonheur, from a watercolor study for *The Horse Fair,* 1867.

For Maxine and Victor Kumin

Contents

The Horse Fair

My skirts would have been a great hindrance, making me
conspicuous and perhaps calling forth unpleasant remarks.
. . . Thus I was taken for a young lad, and unmolested.
—Rosa Bonheur

∽ 1

Found out, identified astride
the chestnut, head tilted
in the manner of the rearing

grey Percheron, you are
Rosa Bonheur disguised as one
of the handlers,

cross-dressed in a blue smock,
center of the painting.
You are performing a fantasy

of belonging
to a genre-scene that admits
none of your sex

and now the art history
that permitted you
to remain invisible

finds you androgynous
where horses bristle
at their restraining tack.

∾ 2

There is in every animal's eye a dim image and gleam of
humanity, a flash of strange light through which their life
looks out and up to our great mystery of command over
them.
—John Ruskin

She would not see them as subservient.
She painted the tarsal joint of the hind leg
for forty years, perfecting its voluted spring.
She knew the Arabian horse to be of porphyry, granite, and sandstone;
she knew the English stallion Hobgoblin, veined with seawater.
She knew anatomical science predicted movement;
thus, in trousers and boots, through the slaughterhouses and stockyards
and livestock markets, a small woman with cropped hair passed.
She knew the Belgian, her dense ossature, wattage of the livid eye,
oscillation of gait, the withheld stampede gathering
in the staunch shoulder for the haulage of artillery.
She would not picture subservience.

◌ 3

The taxonomies enclose and divide
Rosa, lover of science, Rosa, lover of Nathalie and Anna
I am she who asked permission to dress
as a man and had my physician countersign

for reasons of health so I could go forth
into my own country and abroad to study
Scottish sheep and oxen at The Falkirk Fair
I drew their bodies swimming

across the firth at Loch Leven
where drovers in small boats guided
the great beasts struggling up the banks
their sleek heads rose dripping

~ 4

Mlle. Rosa paints almost like a man.
—Théophile Thoré

The oxen configure an immense mute horizon
with the bunkers of their bodies.

Lustrous in the sun they furrow
the ground and plough their shadows under.

Across sienna trenches, uptilted,
they labor two abreast, fissures of skin

greased with oil. Headdresses of horns point.
This was her choice: heavy blade at the end

of the beam, draft teams dwarfing the human
figure, tiny as a painted lead soldier.

~ 5

I have a veritable passion, you know, for this unfortunate race
and I deplore that it is disappearing before the White
usurpers.
—Rosa Bonheur

Cody sold *the unfortunate race* to England and France
as the *real* west in *actual scenes*
of slaughters in which he bragged he had taken part
we do not know—the facts
surrounding his life are uncertain

but not the promotional posters with Red Shirt
and Rosa Bonheur
given permission to draw in the thirty-acre field
where performers camped
between staged conquests Cody presented as *civilizing*

A chronicle of despair said Black Elk who joined
The Rough Riders to mend the broken
hoop of history   In the portrait Bonheur painted
Cody rides a white horse, sits tall in fringed buckskin
on playbills and postcards

They say he was not entirely pleased with the likeness
and had his head repainted

I strove to comprehend the soul
of Fathma, my lioness
reclining with her on a straw mat
studying her eye in many drawings

I stocked my stables with Icelandic
ponies, goats and yaks
Elk roamed the grounds and sometimes I
was summoned by the Empress

as I worked from a plaster cast
of a gazelle or a stuffed hawk
or played with Boniface the monkey
who liked to take my hand and walk

The taxonomies enclose and divide
They said I was a Jew
from Bordeaux
and called me Rosa Mazel-Tov

before I died famous on the lip
of the twentieth century
Numerous the forged engravings, the collaborating
dealers, the pirated prints

of *The Horse Fair,* the notebooks
carrying my studio stamp and the stories
of a critic discovering me
in a frock coat, trousers, spurs, queer hat.

ॐ 8

Nine horses running in a cadenced score,
their unshod hooves thresh the wheat and the thresher's whip
like a high note on the unfinished canvas.

An immense dream of balance, gallop, and pivot—
without bridle or harness—
the picture hung for thirty years in the atelier.

She wanted to show the fire that blows
from the horses' nostrils, and the driven herd mutinous, rising
and falling along the enclosure of the thresher's will

into the foundry of weight and motion
where metal melts and pours into horse.
Dangerous as fission the arson of their turning;

tails flare behind obdurate haunches, chests brace in disavowal.
She painted the intelligence of dished faces resisting—
her life's project their refusal.

One

Ephemera

The snake, alphabet of one glide, swims
with its keepsake head, periscoping, and then

we lose it in the pond grass, lashed
among the bottom-feeders. Pocketing goggles,

my gaze tends pineward, to the driest sky
in twenty years (also passing, rain predicted),

a month of sun days. In Fairbanks, all-night baseball
and a picnic breakfast Alaskan-style. Someone's

driving south, to Anchorage, in that luscious uplift
that here will linger long enough for us

to get a sunburn, to get down, to get stung,
to get the hang of happiness and get going.

Get the picture? I do, but just for the moment,
which is why I want it monumental, equestrian,

astride, however I can get it. What's
passing is June, another: peony's scent; postcards

from the lower forty-eight. The frog I trod sprang back
intact, all its receptors set on July.

Life Forms

When a whale rolls ashore
the villagers know a drowned person
is coming home
who may have started life
as a halibut, shucked tail and fins
for a musher's lot.
If she's going to die soon,
a woman may hear the owl call her name.
A screech owl is a person
punished for speaking out of turn.
I didn't know the canoe
in the museum
had been a two-headed sea serpent
the Kwakiutl fed with seals.
I didn't know that raven's wings
could open to reveal
a human head.
A woman washing in a stream refused
to come when her husband called.
Her leather apron slapped the shore,
became a tail. She grew thick fur
and slipped from her marriage
disguised as a beaver.
We stopped at Nenana to place our bets
on the exact minute of the ice breakup.
I wanted to see the clock that stops
when the ice goes out.
I wanted to see the salmon-man
who pumps gas at the filling station,
forced into the human world
after leaping upriver.

The Wood Lot

for Victor Kumin

In the farmhouse, early morning,
you review the list of chores
tacked to the post. They vary by season,

site, number of hands needed,
number of trips, machinery
and vehicles. Tasks fall into invisible

sub-categories—the urgent,
the accidental, the rock-bound.
We walk uphill, you're explaining

citizenship, your passion for the civic work
that builds a library, a community,
a two-hundred-year-old stone wall.

We spend an hour stacking wood,
a companionable chore, good for two,
you tell me, never one alone.

Alone, the stacker will grow careless, miss
the logs' listing tendency, forget to throw
halves aside for supporting ends. You shim

unsteady places as we go, selecting
pieces for the trim, crisp line
that gives us room for another row.

You are love's year-round
caretaker, and by your example I understand
the artfulness of love's responsibilities.

Phaeton

for Maxine Kumin

He sees the light cart in the paddock,
isn't thinking of the time he spooked a month ago—
the cart half-hitched, the gate unlocked—
and you held on. Today he's calm,

standing quietly as you thread the traces through the
footman's loop and ask him to back up. I stand
by his Arab head, masked in mosquito netting, and then
join you in the seat that substitutes, today, for his back.

Easy in your hands, he trots up the road, ears alert
to your voice, the encouraging praise, the clucks that urge him
past laziness when the hill steepens. Your hands know
the give and take of the canter, the sweet compromise

that adjudicates his power and your will. In our helmets,
under these summer trees, we are as safe as we will ever be.

Solstice Bay

Equidistant from origins and destinations, I balanced like the sun on the ecliptic,
      the obligations of love and work remote as the Amish
boy in his single suspender, ploughing with a team of Percherons at the edge
      of my mind. The pleasure came from feeling

 hemispheric, half of me voting to move, half of me voting to stay put.
      I could use the word *zenith* and really mean it,
looking out from the vast, unknowable field
      of middle age to the upper reaches of the sky,

still in a body. Grateful for a body that could feel
      this simple balance, some might call *indifference,*
a form of moderation unfamiliar to the angry and ambitious.
      The lesser gods of envy and pettiness rested up

in their stalls, never far, chewing. Fresh sawdust underfoot
      and a fan in the barn kept them clean and cool
as the sun rose. It always goes like this: we wake one day—
      undeterred, ahistorical—and then the phone rings,

just when we're feeling epistolary. That's why I wanted to
      linger over breakfast, to listen to the mild
conversation, everyone still sleepy, to drift inside this shapely
      calm within the sweet music of their plans.

        ❧

As a child, I saw the way time shimmered
      around a date on the calendar, the tug and drift,
the disappearing and bobbing up, the surprise of finding the number
      nearing, the impossible, incremental creep

as it hovered. In this way, we practice growing old,
            exercising the muscles that have to give.
When my friend's son Sam asks if he will die
            I know he sees his child's flesh

in the scarred birch trees, in the horse's weeping eye
            covered with flies, in the bodies of women.
He recognizes his body in the old dog's body,
            and he feels great sympathy for all

that will happen to his body and to the bodies
            he loves. "I think I'll be ninety-six
when I die," he says clearly. At Solstice Bay,
            the longest day includes in perfect equilibrium

a remembering and a forgetting, no need
            to make a fuss of time finding the leaves
in the form of light, though we do, we make
            something of it—anything—again and again.

Dylan's Fault

My students refuse to write
about the darkness in their lives.
We want to be happy, one chimes in.
Even the smart girl is with them this time.
Show us joy, she taunts.

And now I can't think
of a single joyful poem I'd like
to assign them, to prove I'm not
a depressing geek and know
how to have a good time. Instead,

I ask them to turn to page 58, I can't help
myself, they asked for it: *Fern Hill.*
The smart girl volunteers to read aloud
and does so in the flat voice of the smart-bored.
It's a trap, someone shouts from the back,

The descriptive detail is just a ploy
to lead us on. One boy rises to fire, pointing
a long finger at me. The class quiets.
Dylan Thomas was just like all you poets!
He knew all along he was going to die!

The Donor

for Richard Mihelcic

He was the largest man I'd ever seen.
Sun glittered behind him on new leaves. He shook
our hands. "My son was just a college kid who turned
special at the end; I learned, praise God, so much. . . ."
Who is this man? I wondered in his plush D.C. office,

where we sat rapt before his story like students,
not teachers on a fund-raising errand,
part condolence call. I remembered the thin
young man and his poems that lacked concrete detail,
while his father hurried on, steering us

through the molecular compositions
that would not stay the stridor issuing
from the boy's lungs, the streptozotocin
that wiped out insulin-producing cells,
the boy's heroic sadness, season of gurneys.

Had my father ever unburdened himself
to a stranger? After my sister took her life
he stared, spent, from a room darkened by shame,
silent. The donor divested himself of secrets,
made public his desperate transactions:

in the sub-basement at Hopkins, on the Volga River in winter,
he wrapped his boy in a blanket, in a nineteenth-century
novel, for a twenty-first century procedure.
His sentences coursed into Chekhovian time, while I
pondered the carriage driver in "The Lament,"

overcome by his son's death, seeking someone
to listen to his tale. In the end, he tells his horse
his threnody. And though we were strangers
to him, Matthew's father described how the doctors broke
his son's ribs to get at his heart, how, wasted

by liver failure, he hung on, every antibiotic
active against tumors blackening his body.
He conjured a language in which machines conversed,
wept, asked forgiveness, obsessed with the telling
details. And when he saw we were crying,

he asked our permission to continue
through the damaged corridors
through the Valley of the Shadow of Death and up
to the ICU and the months of shunts
and feeding tubes, to the empty stomach

at the end of the world. The sub-strata of menace.
There, he named names—doctors compassionate and harsh—
who bought Matt time while he was dying. Once, when the boy was close
to death, he fed him, for the taste, chocolate
 ice cream. Then pumped it out.

"My son was just a kid grown magnificent
by dying." He wiped his brow. "Thanks for coming."
This father, shot through with love and grief,
secured his son's ordeal in us, transfusion
of words. The donor's money will fund a prize

each year. And what shall we do with this fearful
story of one man's suffering but shine and polish it
with our own additions and subtractions? What shall we subsidize
with our sorrows after the morning meeting,
all of our assets liquid as tears?

Two

Raccoon

With his two hands
    covering his two eyes
        he prays in the middle of the road

over the clump of fur and bone
    that was himself.
        He looks like my old *zayde*

in the synagogue
    two decades ago
        ashamed for his poverty.

Comedian of the hard frost,
    deft champion of screw-on tops,
        more than once we met

over the garbage of daily life—
    you poised on the proscenium
        of a metal lid,

me caught in the isosceles
    of an upstate porch light.
        For forty years my grandfather stitched

linings into women's suits
    under a searchlight the shop foreman hung
        over the old man's head.

Sometimes he slapped his son with his hat
    when he got home and cursed his boss
        for making him sew on the Sabbath.

Not even a coat will be made of you,
      brother raccoon, you who did not outlive
          this year's bachelor's buttons and marigolds,

who secured whatever flesh
      you could find and made your way
          dragging your black-ringed tail

across the collaborating streets at dawn
      where the local truckers
          in their shiny rigs stop at nothing.

Autumn Song

∂ 1

Tawny stars spin around our shoulders—
harvest and chaff, familiar and contested,

dual, silver-tongued as the undersides—losing
moisture but not just *yet,* momentarily

shot with imperial purple, cardinal, gold.
As they turn toward their dying, they turn

ornamental, the way my grandmother embellished
the cardiac wing with her onyx eyes,

her pewter hair, her immigrant's
fractious love for this country.

∂ 2

Tumbling and clicking across the asphalt lot,
leaves sound like a child walking a stick

between the fence's slats, a counterplot.
In the gutter, the bright and the dull

coil in a loose skein, the summer past seined up
for us to gather and burn in autumn's

recursive regime. Each year, after the Days of Awe,
after the prayers and atonement, my grandmother

returned to the deciduous world, lustrous
as an oiled leather bridle.

≈ 3

In the wide silence behind the house
the owl calls, pioneering; another,

from the pines, rakes the dust. They inscribe
a grid of cries in the riven air,

their capital predation and flight. Tomorrow,
rinsed light on the roof of the toolshed,

the last October morning glories will
twist like lavender twine alongside shards

of bone and fur. On the ground, the first
chestnuts scatter, bursting their prickly husks.

The Keeper

In the chicken coop,
two bloody birds lay in the dirt, feathers
scattered. She looked up, hoping to sight
an owl or hawk in the leaves. A rattling
from the hen house, and six birds flapped out.
She knelt and peered into the darkness, two eyes

glowed. Came closer. When she rose to back
out of the enclosure, the creature snarled,
crimson gums like the blade of a sawfish.
As she tells it, she knew he was rabid and turned and ran
up the porch, but he followed, summoning
his disordered energy. She slammed the door

just as he wedged his snout against the frame.
A country woman, she knew the ways of animals,
but he climbed the Adirondack chair and splayed himself
against the window, scratching and tapping the glass
to find a way to her. She said he went methodically
from window to window, and with his prehensile hands

he tried the locks, he searched for a breach in the screens,
he circled the house and found the sump pump and followed
its snaking length into the basement.
There, he commenced to open crates of family china,
he smashed the Mason jars and sampled last summer's pickles,
he uncovered her great-grandmother's tooled chest

and held the old garments to his face. She loaded the gun
and found him crouching in a soft heap
of flannel and cashmere, panting, his purple eyes
squinting at his assailant who stood in a nimbus
of light before she fired. The worst part,
she said, was killing the chickens.

It was law in the county, so she shot them
one by one, until her own quiet yard ran with blood,
and burned them along with the hen house.
What had he wanted with her aprons and sweaters?
Public Health carried him out in an old smock
stitched with a ragged, honeycombed text.

Wants

Two Jewish kids among Protestants,
   we knew to stand up for the other,
      though we wanted something we each couldn't get:

I wanted the smart, athletic girls
   on the varsity squad, their confidences, their blue book bags
      leaning against my leg in study hall;

you wanted to be thin, to get a Gentile boyfriend,
   a normal boy from public school who'd make you swoon.
      Nights, you tapped a long finger on the cannister of pot

you hid in your dresser, and we laughed until I got paranoid or sad.
   Lighten up, you'd say. *Soon we'll be out of this hell hole.*
      When your brother came home, he rooted for money

in every room, finally jumped you for your wallet. *No!* you screamed
   as he ran—high on meth—to his Triumph, taking
      the bills and tossing your wallet on the lawn.

King of shopping centers, your grandfather *made more money*
   in a year than most make in a lifetime, my mother said.
      Your brother wrecked three cars, you went to diet camp.

We didn't speak for twenty-five years,
   and then you tracked me down. How our dead from that town
      have accumulated, Ellen! So many dead! The German

Jews who turned away from their Russian cousins
   lie in the ground with them now. They join the shopping center Jews
      and the tailor Jews, the Jews driven mad, like my sister,

and your dreadful mother whose money came to you,
     who would have preferred her love, instead. Your brother—
       tracks up his arms, houses gone, deficits actionable—borrows

against the estate, sues the trustees.
     What else is new? A second husband and a son, the quiet view
       from the window, nothing I would have expected of you.

You can't always get what you want, Mick Jagger sang.
     We did not know our history and class
       would stockade us, until illness or bad luck.

Years ago, in blue tunics, the volleyball captains chose sides
     and we suffered to watch the choosing, to see
       who would be picked last. Sometimes you. Sometimes me.

Elegy for a Secular Man

❧ 1

He lived in the days he fabricated
    with *retablos* and *santos* and painted Acoma pots
        he bought in 1951 at the Santo Domingo Feast Day
           a six-hour drive from Taos over dirt
              with his lovers, men uncertain
                  about Henry and his falling-down adobe

and his plan to dwell in that dry conquered country
    Anglo among the spirits of the Basket Makers
        among the Penitente and the suspicious
           Like the forsaken desert broken into angular planes
              he wore his brokenness his rage his respect his secularism
              he drove the Bookmobile to every parish in the county

❧ 2

I know who you are
    and I know who I am
        I'm just not sure where we are
           he said in the nursing home
           under the fluorescence
              He slowly pulled his wrist-
              watch to his face and said
                  seven-thirty
                but one isn't certain
              if that means morning or evening
              He nodded to the window
        it only matters in that world

ɜ 3

Henry watched from his aluminum folding chair
    as they danced he studied their beaded moccasins
and heard the bells and tortoise shells and deer hooves
    clank and sing against the men's bodies
streaked with white paint and sweat

Among the dancers moved the clowns who stooped to tie
    a headdress or massage a dancer's cramp
Like mothers they shepherded the dancing children
    one lost   one out of line   feminized by their function
never losing their great power said Henry

ɜ 4

In the painting of the procession,
storm clouds bear down
like blocks of ingots—

gauntlet gray, gunmetal gray.
And the false dusk almost
shadows the foregrounded hills,

pewter under snow. There, the cortege
winds, serpentine, as figures follow
one another like pack ponies,

over poor footing,
in the narrow space
the painter reserved for mourners,

unaware of the hole he cut
in the marbled cloud cover
where a spot of blue burns through.

5

When his hearing went he shouted *The liver is the most diseased part*
    of the animal in line at Furr's cafeteria before the opera
        I'll have the liver, please he crooned The smell of sage blew
            through the open windows after *The Magic Flute*
                What's the matter with this company? he roared
                    Their voices get fainter every year

He lived in rooms made complex by the patterns
    of Navajo rugs named for old trading posts
        Two Grey Hills Crystal Germantown
            cochineal stripes draped chair and bed
                cobalt crosses pictograph of cow and horse
                    saddle blanket stained with use

6

Diapered and sweet-smelling he lay
on the hospital bed *This isn't exactly the Waldorf, honey*
he said, humming an ostinato

O my drag queen my Communist my Jew
We know the dignity in self-effacement
the mockery the erasure the devastating remark

Now your brain cannot control your bowels
I pull the diaper from your ankles and leave you
on the toilet   I will bring the attendant

to clean you up while I wait in the lobby
learning the illiberal limits of my love
in this afterlife of the body

In Praise of the Basset Hound

This unlovely dog, with warts, and a terrible stink
common to the breed, legless as a walrus, teaches me
to pursue my life with devotion. Steadfast enthusiast
of fisher cat and vole, she relies now almost entirely on scent
and sings her hound's song of pleasure when we come
close enough for her to hear her name.
In snow above her shoulder, she tracks our skis,
when all we can see is her metronome tail
tipped in black, sweeping the horizon a mile back.
We keep her, incontinent, in an old shed behind the farmhouse,
a wire fence around her run. Warm days, nose in the air,
she sits like an old retiree in the sun, listening
to warblers build their spring nests.
Her warts ooze, her eyes rain green phlegm. Still,
I kiss her and hold her against my breast,
she who whelped twelve litters before someone
took pity and bought her from the breeder.
Never permitted to lick hand or face, she will not
disgrace her training and extend her tongue in play,
though I offer my cheek. Daily, she shows me
the meaning of character, loping painfully
on swollen paws. I apply salve to her scaley folds,
croon over her. Who among us has not been
moved by the magnificence of mute
creatures in their abundant, dying skin?

Dog-God

To the railroad tracks at the bottom of summer
where weeds flourished, I return.

Flat-chested girl in a soiled T-shirt, I liked
the gully's privacy and the rank smell there

where I found dimes flattened by trains and milky
marbles, and once a rusty knife.

I must have reached for a trinket
in the grass when the collie's narrow muzzle

came close, the tricolored wedge of her head a foreign flag.
My first thought—*I have to return her*—I pushed aside

and stood still so she would stay and I could touch
the rich black hair that shone on her. She didn't run away.

To test her, I jogged up the hill and she followed, friendly,
like the TV dog, and when she sat, I sat, flushed with my amazing

luck, and wondering how long it might last, the whole
summer, maybe. I stroked her white breast and said *Scotland* out loud.

She cocked her head as if I'd conjured, with a charm, her name
or home, or a place we'd visit that afternoon. At a stream,

she drank, and the sound of her lapping excited a new desire
to master what is beautiful and guileless and mute.

The Abandoned Meander

I walked the mesa, with its spiny barbs
and lonely desert owls, knowing I'd come to the end
of something, maybe myself.

Without those good citizens, the trees,
I shed my good belt and the chore of belonging,
and ran in the mornings, shouting to the prairie dogs.

I passed through the hands of a woman,
unencumbered, who passed through mine.
On the controversies in town, I offered no opinions.
My money circulated in grocery and laundry.

In horseshoe canyons, on volcanic rock, the shield bearer,
lightning arrows, the dancing figure with corn.
Handprints on black basalt matched my hand.

Like the rain clouds passing the talus cliffs,
I meant nothing, I was forgettable, free
as the stray dogs I fed before they crossed the sandbars
or bathed in the Rio Grande.

When I cooked my dinner, I stroked the adobe
wall crumbling against my cheek, a living building
breathing and suffering and burning.

Now, when I think of that country
I smell sagebrush on the wind—deft priestess
raking the mesa into swirling lines of dust.

Mid-life

Almost everyone at art camp wears
a full head of dark hair. Mornings,
they casually allude to parties, getting to sleep at three or four.
As usual, there are a few great beauties who
treat me like an older sister—hip but no
all-nighters. What happened to my competitive spirit?
My rakish scarf? Like an old man, I miss my
basset hound.

Back home, my Mountain Laurel creates curb appeal,
my mailbox salutes, a sturdy citizen on the road.
Last month I felt great communion with my neighbors
as we all cursed and mowed. Then we hauled
our recycling bins to the street in unison, we made
the collective squeal of our village.

Still, I like these young people,
some of whom still read poetry
and smoke cigarettes.
We share a taste for the linen suits I found
along Mass Ave., when I lived in a studio
in Cambridge, city of brick and rescued greyhounds.
Restless, I didn't know that wanting
was already a kind of having.

Today over lunch I will have an argument with myself
and enjoy it thoroughly, taking both sides,
gesturing and furrowing my brow.
Then it will grow so quiet
in this glade of light and leaves that I might
mistake myself for a bear, a deer.

Late Words for My Sister

You did not want to remember
  with me how he raged up the stairs
    unbuckling the black leather

strap we called *the belt*.
  How our four thin legs danced
    up and down on the bed like

the jointed limbs of marionettes
  while the burning lariat of his anger
    seared our legs; how his face blazed and his eyes

glowed as he took the whip back in a tight
  circle to strike again. And again. We begged him to stop.
    Remember? And when he relented, panting like an animal

that has run a great distance, he paused, and we could see
  the sweat on his lip and under his arms. He hung there,
    his bulk suspended from his shoulders

by a power greater than he, and as we crept past him
  he slapped me, hard across the face, sparing you
    that humiliation

because you were weak and the youngest
  and had only followed my example into evildoing.
    I tried to make myself small, to pass him, or no,

I'm remembering wrong. Maybe I sneered. Maybe
  I had not yet learned to cower before the bully,
    to bare my neck, to admit when I had lost.

How surprised you would be to see him now,
    an old man checking the price
        of milk at the supermarket against

the price in his head. The difference
    is a conundrum, a fracture in continuity,
        the way his daughters broke from his plan.

Three

In the Days of Awe

for Abbe, Sally, and Joseph

ॐ I *Amidah*

Hear my personal prayer, *the words of my mouth and the meditation*
of my heart that I may find a way back through love
In the hospital room packed in blood-soaked cotton the new mother lay
animal-exhausted technicians whisked the child away in the first
hours there was fear O teach me to withhold judgment

of the one who took my place who said *yes* when I said *no*
whose days opened to the child when my days foreclosed
she who conceived of joy where I imagined the crossbar
against my chest subjugation of family life the double
harness the never ending tasks the clamp and vise

ॐ II *Shofar*

The *shofar* blasts birthday of the world of our dominion
over nature in the Kingdom of the Lord our God Ruler
of the Universe Then why am I weeping into this tissue?
What is this child to me who refused to stay and raise him?
What is this broken covenant, this yoke?

ॐ III *Tashlikh*

By a small stream as is customary
we cast into the water with its drift
of leaves our quarrels like stones our envies
and resentments *O Lord You do not maintain anger*
but delight in forgiveness

43

~ IV *Aleinu*

You take me down to the nursery to see
Joseph in his little cap of many colors
with his jaundice and his brisk efficient keepers
Will you be kind? *Cleanse my mind of wickedness*
Teach me to attain a heart of wisdom

In the synagogue the families praise *all fruitbearing trees*
and cedars all wild beasts and cattle I watch a woman
and her teenage daughter confer lean into each other
They hold the *mahzor* between them their mouths shape the beautiful
Hebrew I do not know how to read except in transliteration

~ V *Teshuvah*

Turn from evil and do good the Psalmist says turning
Round the turn turn the key clock the turn turn in time
time to turn words into footsteps to lead the young colt to the field
to turn from the old year the old self You are ready
to turn and be healed only face only begin

~ VI *Amidah*

Inscribe him in the Book of Life for Your sake living God
She opened up the book of her body again and again
She would not stop trying though I mocked her a year
ended and a year began I had no imagination for family life
inhabiting sadly that place for years

inhabiting sadly that place for years   with me   who chose
to keep my faith with those who sleep in dust   she chose
against the quiet house and noiseless rooms she chose
to bear her mortal woman's share and split her life in two
or three or four   she said *I know what you want   I want more*

ᐍ VII *Avinu malkeinu*

Avinu malkeinu inscribe us in the Book of Deliverance
Avinu malkeinu inscribe us in the Book of Merit
Avinu malkeinu inscribe us in the Book of Forgiveness
Sarah beseeched God for a child and brought forth Isaac
And Sally brought forth Joseph   *Amen*

A voice commands the lightning that cleaves stones
A voice shatters stately cedars
A voice twists the trees and strips the forest bare
The devout say *In your love for your neighbor will you find God*
They say *Days are scrolls Write only what you want remembered*

ᐍ VIII *Kedushah*

We believe that God abides in mystery   in a diaspora of dust
in the obsessive   the compulsive   the disordered   in the lonely
in the bosses   in the unendurable   in the technological
and pharmaceutical failures   in the very old
in the newborn   in memory   in kindness   in acts of lovingkindness

We believe that God abides in the unfit in those unshielded
by luck or faith and by bad luck made abject by the unctuous
I believe in the uncomputerized and the demoralized
the belittled and benumbed gazing like dumb beasts
like my sister groping mid-seizure back to speech

45

℘ IX *Mourner's Kaddish*

Bless my sister who could not endure bless her failure to thrive
and bless my parents in their magnificent witness
Sanctify this *Day of Remembrance   Grant them peace*
from the clichéd language of condolence cards Be merciful to those
who passed *Your blessed days* in a curtained room of shame

In the public place in the hall outfitted with a simple ark
the mourners stand *Whom shall I dread?* we ask with our private
dreads on our civic faces We are an assembly of stunned
children called to recite *Yit-gadal ve-yit kadash shmei raba*
There is always someone to mourn Look around

℘ X *The Fast of Yom Kippur*

Look around the congregation atones we certify regret
we recall our transgressions and those who transgressed against us
Where is my milk? Joseph cries and she feeds him The Torah
teaches repentance I remember my *zayde*, a shrunken man
at the front of the *shul* fasting   By the last *Aleinu* he could not stand

My father brought smelling salts the son who did not know
the prayers sat with his father *His life was one long prayer*
to the hereness of God   On the maternity floor food and flowers
Choose life! shouts baby Joseph tightly bound in a cotton blanket
I'm afraid it's time to go says the kind nurse after visiting hours

℘ XI *Selihot*

The days of women and men are as grass.
They flourish as flowers in the field.
The wind passes over them and is gone,
and no one can recognize where they grew.

46

ᐱ XII *Amidah*

Inscribe for me a childless life   O lift me
to the Book of Many Forms that I might find another way
to honor my father and mother   their agony of bereavement
Let me understand the girl child I was beloved as Joseph in his coat
of many colors, favored by his father hated by his brothers

and by his brothers thrown into the pit Then to live among strangers
in Egypt far from family   Bind me to these friends and to this child
that I may learn my true relation to the people of this story
Sanctify difference and refusal bless
the lesbians the child with two mothers   *Amen*

Four

The Unnamed City

In the blue light it's impossible to tell the addict from the ex-
addict, the bag with the used works from the bag with the clean syringe.
Like monks, social worker and junkie bend at the waist
and bow before each other, as if to sanctify the meeting.
Now it's raining and we could be anywhere—a dusty plaza
in central Mexico where, on Easter, men in masks with gigantic
noses enter the church. According to tradition, the masked Jews
steal Christ while believers pelt them with fruit.
This has gone on, we are told, for hundreds of years: pestilence
and ritual, ceremony and the illegal transport of drugs.
In the neutral voice of the telecast we are informed of cities
where *la clinica* operates in the open; this unnamed city
is not one of them. In this unnamed city infected needles claim
ten lives a day, but everyone turns out for fiesta,
and their costumes are beautiful, and their children know
the passion play, the moment to hurl the fruit at the Jews.
When the shower is over, the addicts crawl
from their cardboard bunkers. The cameraman feels sorry but he must
hold the camera steady. In a blue office, the social worker explains
that soon it will be summer, and the homeless and runaways
will mingle in the parks as if at a great outdoor party,
and the needles, like his Christian love, will pass
from hand to hand like the blankets infected with
smallpox which the conquering army traded for land.

Sisters in Perpetual Motion

Urban wanderers,
      unhoused and unhinged, they are rapt in
            a perpetual motion of paraphernalia

trundling from Kendall to Central, Harvard to Porter.
      One in a gentleman's greatcoat—
            worsted gabardine and fur collar—

holds a sidebar conference with herself, pushes her metal
      shopping cart, argues with the invisible
            censorious judge of Mass Ave.

Parallel to traffic, she retains a centrifugal
      relationship to the lanes she occupies, strides
            away from the main, parent axis of rotation,

abjures public transportation or charity and returns,
      early evening, cold, coincident with those of us
            not charged with a conundrum of streets.

She sleeps in undocumented doorways and on grates and
      in neighborhood parks on benches and propped
            on soiled cushions she pushes.

Sponge of pocked foam bedding. Torn lining of a brown coat.
      Thus I remember my sister, her unbuilt days
            of compulsive walking before she decamped

to clinics and psych wards. Her walkabouts. Her unfettered speech.
       Her terrorist phone calls and the tyranny
           of her jurisdiction: thus, beleaguered,

she engineered a siege and won. *Timber up a frame dwelling,*
      I said. *Explain yourself to yourself.* In the end,
         the cops broke down the door of an empty house to find her.

The Grief of Trees

۞ 1

We returned at night, the autumn landscape
    frozen beneath a white crust.
        In the dark, my lover and I kicked

at lilac boughs overtaken by ice and
    the subdued blueberry bushes,
        and as we kicked the ice yielded

and the rounded limbs sprang back.
    We kicked and unfastened the stooped limbs
        of the chestnut tree from a tent of snow.

And we struck the buried
    laurel bushes to which the leaves still clung,
        and we punted ice from tiny pines.

Our recovered world! How sere and mattering it looked—
    each fork and needle against
        the killing cold and sky.

And from the shed she drew a spade
    and worked her way around the perimeter
        of the place and hacked at the heavy sacks

of wet snow wedged in the brimming branches.
    Above her, the splintered shafts of spruce and fir;
        before her, a hundred severed limbs her length

dented the insolent ice. I imagined that she could drop
    each broken branch into a carafe of water,
        and like ivy, each would grow a transparent root.

54

 2

The next day Beth brought
   her chain saw and five friends hauled
     neatly sawed-off living wood

to the side of the road. She saved
   her birch trees, staying up all night
     to beat them with a broom,

while transformers blew and bursts of light
   stung the sky like bombs. She said the worst part
     was the sound of the breaking trees,

the wheeze before the crack, the quick snap
   of the smaller branches and the aching refrain
     of the trees that slowly opened and split.

In every shop, someone has a story of the storm, a narrative
   of how it broke into her life and how she was alone,
     without power, without phone, just the dog and the kids.

Along the village streets and on the rural roads
   the storied heaps of dismembered oak and elm
     deployed for cordwood, the grief of trees.

You pour fifty pounds of birdseed into the barrel
   and check the feeders. While we were away, a neighbor
     kept them full, and that first morning you woke

to find junco and titmouse and nuthatch and cardinal
   and a new bird feeding above the devastation,
     the evening grosbeak, like the storm, just passing through.

Sad Sestina

for Susanna Kaysen

Today's sadness is different from yesterday's:
more green in it, some light rain, premonition of departures
and the unpacking of books and papers. *It's not a bad thing*
to be sad, my friend Susanna says. *Go with it.* I'm going by foot
into this sadness, the way we go as children into the awful
school day and the hours of cruelty and misunderstanding,

the way we go into family, into the savagery of standing
up for ourselves among siblings and parents, in yesterday's
living room, where secrecy turns to habit and we learn the awful,
unthinkable fact: time twists our days into a series of departures.
When he was mad, my father used to say *Someone's got to foot*
the bills, and I think of him now, this man who knew one thing

for sure: you had to pay your own way, since nothing
came for free in this life. A young dyke, grandstanding
before the relatives, I held my sadness close, one foot
already out the door. Who could believe in yesterday's
homilies while women cruised me, seventeen and hot for departure?
Today's sadness unfurls without drama, without the awful

punishments or reprisals of that house. In its place, the awful,
simple, mystery of human melancholy. Most days, I'd trade anything
to be rid of the blues, accustomed to flight and departure,
strategies that saved my life. Today I'm befriending it, standing
beside my sadness like a pal down on her luck, who knows yesterday
isn't always a good predictor for tomorrow. A rabbit's foot

won't help; when the time comes, it's a question of putting my foot
in the stirrup and riding the sad horse of my body to the awful
little stable at the edge of town. And there to wait while yesterday
has its way with time. Susanna said, *To be sad is not a bad thing,*
and I believe her, as I pull the heavy saddle from the standing
horse and hang the bridle away. Sadness readies for my departure,

and I for hers. In a most unlikely departure
from the ordinary, even the tough butch on a bike will be a tenderfoot
when it comes to goodbyes. We carry on, notwithstanding
all the good times gone and December's awful
cheerfulness. Susanna, if I ever discern something
useful about sadness, I'll wish I'd known it yesterday.

I've put distracting things aside and discovered, underfoot,
no wisdom absent yesterday. Still, a saint would find this awful:
a standing date with change, a season of departures.

Rustic Portrait

for Carolyn

Here is the woodpile, listing a bit under its tarp, a few logs fallen,
and the stump to which she goes, sometimes after dark, with an axe.
Here is the kitchen of cast iron pans, history of garlic, tomatoes and oil.
Here is the midnight mouse, the moon moving across linoleum.

Here is her morning of dogs on the road of corn and winter wheat.

Here is her arm, pouring the seed that draws grosbeak and bunting,
the chickadee who will not leave but sits in her hair.
Now the downy woodpecker arrives for his cage of suet
and now the nuthatch who sees the world upside-down.

Here is her garden, where the spring frog leaps from lettuce to peas,
where she goes to pick dinner, kneels against everyday
torpor before herbs in their fragrant circle of stone,
florets in blue mantles, flourishing.

Here the brief lilacs, there the peonies with their essential ants,
the hungry day lilies, open-mouthed and singing, the blue
delphiniums scaling the season after trillium
and lady-slipper disappear from the edge of the clearing.

Here is the owl who belongs to herself, sending the dark
news of her accession from forest to house.

Here is the rake with its long afternoons of labor
in the gathering dark, the mower that knows retirement is near
when the neighbors set out their harvest of gourds and pumpkin.
Sunflowers feed the finches long after she mulches the rest.

In winter, she enters the field on skis, the younger dog
trotting in her tracks. Small animals dragged the last corncobs
to a clearing, where a frozen deer haunch sprawls in the snow.
Chickadee and titmouse alone now at the feeders.

Here is the woodpile, listing a bit under its tarp, a few logs fallen
and the stump to which she goes, sometimes after dark, with an axe.

The Evidence

The woodpecker troubles bare branches
and disappears with my attention.
Far-flung orbit of energy, she

settles for a moment
but a restless aptitude drives her
hungers, like the engine that powered

my heart toward the kind
and beautiful lovers I failed
to cherish for the momentary

pastures they offered.
I preferred longing to having,
every woman an opportunity

for grief, every date the beginning
of betrayal. I would have married the past
with its shapely stories of sadness. . . .

When I take off my coat, it's winter,
a three-day thaw, and her hands on my skin
are a stranger's. She leads me to my senses,

to laughter, to the stories strangers tell
about themselves in bed, to nothing
but desire which I confuse,

as usual, with love, that frayed rope.
When all the admissible evidence is in
and I'm apprised of my rights in this matter,

I hope to stand with those who love
their lives in time to live them,
bravely, between kisses, beneath stars.

Sonnet to the Imagination

In early March, I watch you sleep, your mouth
open, as if surprised to find yourself
a few hours of rest. I imagine you, a little girl
in New Haven, learning your Hebrew, squirming
under the floodlight of your parents' gaze
the way an only child absorbs the family
depression and rage. You were already
falling in love with revolution, her language
and arguments, her women and children, her Algerias,
her Santiagos. The decades of politics and travel
and lovers became us. Now, I want your mouth
on my mouth and wonder where this wanting will lead
if we let it wander, darling, as I wonder who
you will be after my imagination has ravished you.

Harvest Girl

She has parleyed her summer work
        into autumn leisure and stretches in the sun,
                boots propped on a tin bucket,

her pleasure uncomplicated as the junco's
        sated with seed. She wears my neighbor's
                red flannel shirt and faded jeans,

old leather gardening gloves
        open at the seams, and a pumpkin head carved
                with my neighbor's mouth. One stuffed shoulder

leans toward a wooden wheelbarrow
        repainted red and arrayed with straw,
                a bed for mottled goose-necked gourds

dried and hung for rattles and dippers.
        The Butternut and Acorn squash that summered
                on thick vines below the Silver Queen

lounge beside Turk's Turban, a bright tourist
        in red and green stripes. The harvest girl reclines
                and stares at the sheaves of field corn

stacked upright across the road. I've read of harvests
        when the Corn-Spirit fled the field workers
                and took refuge in the barn, hiding

with the last to be threshed. And from the last
        sheaves they made the Corn-Mother doll and
                dressed her in a woman's shirt and carried her

around the village and threw her in the river
and dried her and burned her
and doused the fields with her ashes.

Sometimes a Corn-Maiden effigy, cut and bound
by the youngest, hung in the farmhouse,
a human swag, until the first mare foaled.

In New Mexico, she wore a tablita, festooned
to conjure the tassels of corn, and with her face
painted yellow and red in the colors of maize,

she became the human form of the goddess lamenting
her own death, reborn from the ancient threshings,
her spirit still unsacrificed, indwelling.

Adult Child

Now that my parents are old, they love me fiercely,
and I am grateful that the long detente of my childhood
has ended; we stroll through the retirement community.
My father would like to call the woman who left me
and tell her that I will be a wealthy woman someday.
We laugh, knowing she never cared about money
but patiently taught him to use his computer and program
the car phone. In the condo, my mother navigates
a maze of jewelry, tells me the history of watches,
bracelets, rings, pearls. She says I may sell
most of it, she just wants me to know what's what.
I drive her to the bank where we sign a little card
and walk, accompanied, into the vault, gray boxes
stacked like bodies. *Here,* she says, *are the titles and deeds.*

Yoga

The teacher says
to feel the breath, flowing
up the spine, up the neck

where the vertebrae click
in the teeth of the ratchet
wheel, where concentration

forces spirit upward
on the hinged pawl of perfect
self-control to the

crown of the head.
Next the birds come
with their bits of straw

and fabric and thread.
In the pose of the standing tree
I am a patient bodhisattva

enduring a spring rain
content to forgo enlightenment
and be reborn again and again

in the pose of the downward-
facing dog, inhaling the fecund
April earth with first one

then the other nostril
to practice the sacred shifting
of consciousness from mind

to mind. In this disciplined
exchange of breath
we train for distance

runs at altitude,
incarnations as mountain cats
or Asian trees,

our life's breath finding
a home in every metabolic niche.
Elephant, lotus, monkey,

banyan, we bend boughs
and snouts, balancing the ineffable
as it rolls and pitches

out of these
momentary bodies.

Five

The Triumph of Charlotte Salomon

I was eight years old
                when my mother threw
        herself
from our window at 15 Wielandstrasse

But I knew she really died of influenza
        and flew   from the window
                                an
                                        angel

                                        like her sister
                        Charlotte
        Grunwald   the angel   for whom I am named
        drowned   in 1913

Women at windows, Jewish women—
        . . . and the German doctors
examining bloodlines
                to understand
                        the epidemic in Weimar—

        Who is a child without her mother?
        What is one sister without the other?
        When shall my father find another?
        I shall grow up undercover.

                ❧

Contortionists, twisting
        stories. We bent our names
our professions   our habits of mind
                to the prevailing
                        habit of mind—

Berlin, 1930.
She came into my life as Paula Lindberg, the mezzo-soprano,
and she sang in the bent, sad rooms
and married my father.

Then it was music! Music! Music
though they said my loneliness came
from my mother's family—

Grossmama and Grosspapa cold
in their stiff-backed chairs
their formal clothes   their self-restraint

In my painting   the faceless Nazi herd
parades
to celebrate Chancellor Hitler

Their swastikas
their identical shirts
their slogans   their posters   their power
to turn
my classmates against me

They told us to bring
baptism certificates
In "Race Hygiene" class
my friend had to show
her nose

A Full Jew
I entered the State Art Academy

ॐ

In a dream   I join my father
          and his old friend, Carl   for tea
     Carl—not Jewish, also
          a doctor—asks *Is there something anything*
                    I can do for you?
          (I want to say *yes! Yes!*) But Father, bewildered, laughs.
                    (Doesn't he *know?*)   He assures his old friend
                    we will be fine, no reason
                    for alarm, everything will work out. . . .

ॐ

I loved Wolfson first
          because he loved Paula
as I loved Paula   and second because he made her sing
     (again) as he learned to sing (again) listening
     to the screams   1915
He lost his voice and his mind he became
          his own god
     and then he became mine

On a bench *for Aryans only*
          we kissed
he explained that we are all Orpheus
                    must all go down   into the depths   to rise   I listened
                              to every word I absorbed everything—

You see?   Wolfson was my resurrection
     as the Nazis marched   my life away
          day by day he believed   in himself
     in the triumph of the maimed, the orphaned, the unsigned

painting in the competition I should have won
     but for my name   In 1938 they threw me out of art school

73

My parents put me on a train to France
They promised
to meet me there
ॐ

The night they put me on the train
to Nice   to Grossmama and Grosspapa Grunwald

I had a dream: one of their French retrievers,
a brown dog with curly hair, climbed, dripping
up a riverbank,
a feathered stick
in his mouth
He gave it a quick
snap
and the thing in his jaws
(sickening, cartilaginous)
dropped to the weeds.
The brown dog
plunged down
the slope
into the current,
his muzzle like a gun
in the rusty water.

Then my father
crawled up the reedy incline
and bowed his head
as he did after Sachsenhausen

ॐ

The south of France!   Geraniums in pots on the stairs,
the whitewashed walls of l'Hermitage, salt air!

And Grossmama, scowling, the dark Germany I left,
    doling out her jewelry and cash to the American woman
        hiding a handful of refugees.
Thankless Grossmama!

        I found her
            almost dead, hanging by a noose.

        ◦

        20 March 1940. Grossmama
            jumped from our window.

        ◦

I like to arrive before the sun—
    my eyes before the sun's one eye
before the physics of pattern and deception—

and watch the moments of my past
    accumulate in these paintings   in the sun
whose dominion is not absolute, who must also obey

the clouds and thus is thrall to. . . .

Always reminiscent, always renewing,
    I paint the magical, the rhetorical family,
and how we explain ourselves: historical, psychological. . . .

The light withdraws and the waves turn flat.
    Then with her paint, she brushes the water,
scatters a deceiving light. Capricious sun. Imprisoned sun.

        ◦

I died at Birkenau, crowded into the shower, child of history,

of Zyklon B, of Paula and the suicided Grunwalds.

In the last year of my life, I painted words for every voice

I loved, every deceiving voice that left me—

alone in Nice, digging my way back.

As the Nazis came closer, as the Côte d'Azur swelled

with transports, I painted what memory could not retrieve:

a theater of comprehension, characters moving with and counter

to their desires. On my little stage of despair, I wrote the parts

for every woman of my blood and so found myself there,

among them, in them, the underworld revealed to me as

meaning's last stop. Against the finished music of genocide,

I left the world, my life taken, not given.

Six

Against Silence

Silence is a meadow, guileless, gesturing with indigenous
grasses and wild flowers. Walk into it and the bees rise.
Silence is the thousand-leaved woods in rain,
New England turned jungly, fungal, a grid of humidity
where insects swarm around our martyred heads.

Silence is a game of dodge ball at dusk—
a matter of time until someone knocks you out
of the circle of bodies. I used to sway alone, slow
motion, the ball floating past my chest. Eyes in my hands,
eyes in the small of my back, I could anticipate the blow

and dodge it, schooled in the feint, the simulation.
Silence is the Old City of partition and quarter,
where a colonial fog blots the sun. And all the charm of the regime
hurried away, into museums: see the gold ear plugs?
the short musket with the flaring muzzle?

I want to hear the circular saw rotating at high speed,
excoriation, whine, orchestration of birds. Describe the sexual practices
of several Peruvian cultures. Harpsichord me. Entail me. Depose me.
The dangerous meadow shuts down at night.
The moon, rabbinical, mutters a prayer.

Why We Fear the Amish

Because they are secretly Jewish and eat matzoh on Saturday.
Because they smell us in fellowship with the dead works
of darkness and technology. Because we doubt ourselves.
We find their clothing remorseless; we find their beards unsanitary.
Who among us is not ashamed, speeding, to come upon a poor
horse pulling a cart uphill, everyone dressed the same?
We believe in the state and they believe in the button.

With their fellow Pennsylvanians, the Quakers, they hold noisy pep rallies.
They know the quilting bee, the honey bee and the husking bee
are the only proper activities for women.
Even their horses are thrifty and willing to starve for Christ.
In the Poconos, the men vacation with Hassidim and try on
each other's coats. Back home, no tractors with pneumatic tires.
Pity the child who wants a radio and must settle for a thermos.

When the world shifts to Daylight Savings Time, there's no time
like slow time, to stay out of step. In Standard Time
their horses trot faster than ours, for the Amish
set their clocks ahead. In January, they slaughter the animals.
In March, they go to the sales. In April, they plant potatoes.
In June, they cut alfalfa. In August, they cut alfalfa again.
In October they dig potatoes. In December they butcher and marry.

They modify the milk machine to suit the church, they change
the church to fit the chassis, amending their lives with hooks-and-eyes.
Their dress is a leisurely protest against chairmindedness.
We know their frugality in our corpulence. We know their sacrifice
for the group in our love for the individual. Our gods are
cross-dressers, nerds, beach-bums, and poets. They know it.
By their pure walk and practice do they eye us from their carts.

The Monarchs of Parque Tranquilidad

On the ruins of Synagogue Cheva Bikur, built in 1887,
my neighbors fashioned Parque Tranquilidad
and adorned the gate with blue morning glories,

nimble gymnasts scaling the parallel bars.
I take the brick path to the Spanish Colonial toolshed,
to the bird bath studded with tiles—

our altarpiece—where a wooden Saint Francis
of Assisi oversees all immigrants in the Folk
Art style that dominates visual culture on 4th Street,

as in the commemorative portraits of Emilio and Mike,
painted on the north wall of Casa Mia—
young men who stopped expecting anything and now smile

at stock boys catching a smoke in the park, and single
mothers hurrying their kids to the Catholic school
on Sixth, and the homeless novelist who sets up his portable

typewriter beneath the Ornamental Cherry.
Below their large faces, the muralist wrote,
They are in heaven now.

Today in Parque Tranquilidad, heaven arrives as orange
monarchs, hundreds covering the purple fronds
of the butterfly bush with an involuntary, sexual broadcast

of desire. They linger above the imperial flowers and rush
to embrace them, beating their wings
in a syncopation I cannot fathom, though I stand

for a long time, staring at these migratory,
paper-thin creatures
and the painted faces of the dead boys of 4th Street.

Community Garden, Sixth Street and Avenue B

Into this urban outback
       a child could simply disappear,
              join the feral cats
                     scaling the Rococo jumble

of three-by-fours.
       The tabbies have the leisure
              to peruse the encyclopedic
                     toy store of discards—

kiddie pool, beach ball,
       Star Trek punching bag—
              aloft on wires behind the iron grate.
                     Perpendicular to the forty-foot scaffolding

hangs the plastic horse
       that bucked for a quarter
              at Woolworth's Five-and Dime. Released
                     from memory's corral, she gazes

toward the rearing merry-go-round pony,
       carved in a car barn in Brooklyn, 1925,
              rosettes and tassels decorating the saddle,
                     still galloping to Coney Island.

What gives this tiered tree house
       its wacky, broken wickedness?
              The tawdry and the classical hydroplane
              the late September morning

and I cannot, for once, sprint past
      this pyramid of junk, this towering irony
            without noticing Dumbo, mouth full of shark teeth,
           sailing into the cartoon sky.

Midnight at the Third Street Sculpture Garden

Calcified looms, the rib cages
of giant cats
shine in the moonlight.

This is how the dead
return: costumed children knock at your door,
bones transparent.

Plaster spinal columns—
fused mid-motion, Pompeian—
expose a violent

city's burial. Someone has pillaged the headstones,
urns, potsherds, coins, ash, and left
only the vertebrae to guide

the urban anthropologist.
Like her, I stand at the bars,
drawn to the white

throne on the black grass,
a phosphorescent
electric chair.

Above me, a lunette ornaments the gates,
the sculptor punning the lunacy
of walking at an hour when the gypsum skeletons

become a spectral zoo—
creatures firked and flensed until
this part of Third Street appears

funereal, a ghost town
of shades and phantoms. And I'm
a headless traveler

galloping home, one hand cold
on my wallet of illusions, the other
frozen to the heavy bag of hope.

The Liz Christy–Bowery Houston
Garden

Two thousand varieties of plants grow in this garden
where the child on her back, conversing with the leaves,

suddenly laughs. A patchwork of light spangles
the ecstatic movements of her limbs,

as she waves and kicks at the sky.
I watch a Green Guerilla harvest tomatoes; another

tidies an orchard of cherry, peach and plum trees.
Before their industry, I feel my unemployment

is a disfigurement, not the sweet luxury I'd planned.
Because I mistook her for a normal child

and am embarrassed by her enormous teeth and
little howls, because she reminds me of my sister

and the epilepsy that took her from the row house streets
of childhood to the corridors of strange clinics,

I must accept my day's accomplishment:
gratitude to the volunteer who placed this child

on a tarp, by the fish pond, and shame
at my heart's refusal to acknowledge

the many forms of neglected beauty
with which we might identify, from which we run.

Angels of the Lower East Side

Chico paints the dead of the East Village.
Like God he shows his hand but not his face.
On my street he left us Lilal, hurled from a meteor,
swaddled in the flag of Puerto Rico against a brick galaxy
painted black-and-white. *He couldn't support his habit*

the stock boy tells me. *Killed himself.*
Lilal in a swirling halo, from his eternal place
on the wall of his father's bodega, knows
I'm new here, winks at me behind the enchilada cart,
says *Soon you'll be Puerto Rican,* though I miss the synagogue

that became Iglesia Pentecosto del Divino Maestro
and wander the streets the way I traipsed the ghetto in Venice
in search of Italy's deported Jews. Out of respect
for their friend's son, the 4th Street card players set up the game
where Lilal can oversee their bids, where Chico strides,

invisible Holy Ghost in his gallery of angels.
Next to his portrait of Princess Diana, he painted Elisa,
the child *killed by her mother's boyfriend.* Word on the street
says the city's to blame and the caseworker who failed
to act on complaints. Elisa wears a pink parka, she has

olive skin, the somber eyes and dark hair of the revolutionary
she might have become, standing with the tall
nationalist in his black beret, long raincoat and heavy glasses,
hawking the worker's paper in Spanish outside the supermarket,
rain dripping down his face. In the subway,

wiping his glasses, his pile of unsold papers beside him,
he reminds me of my old friends selling *The Militant*, 1969.
On Houston Street, the young Latina singer, Selina, glances
away, suspicious of her manager, her maid, her fans.
Taken out by someone in her own production company.

We're standing by the liquor store, three doors down
from Iglesia San Isidro y Leandro, another church
that used to be a *shul*. He's waiting for the 14 Bus,
I'm waiting for Elisa and Selina to stop
insisting on their tragedies. I'm waiting for Chico

to explain Diana in expensive pearls against the glittering
background of stars. Chico says *Think of her sons*
and hightails it to the Williamsburg Bridge.
Why can't I escape Diana's bright teeth or forget
Elisa's pink coat, Selina's pursed red lips?

Lilal says *The dead will always be with us—*
in the Jews who inhabited these streets, in those who perished
from typhus, in the violence of the father, in the violence of the tenement,
in the removal of the Star from the round window, in the violence of crack,
in the florid graffiti, in the faces painted on these walls.

Notes

"The Horse Fair": For scholarship on the life and work of nineteenth-century painter Rosa Bonheur, I am indebted to Dore Ashton, Denise Hare, and James Saslow, whose work informed this poem. Quoted passages are from *Rosa Bonheur,* by Dore Ashton and Denise Hare (New York: Viking, 1981). Used by permission of Viking Penguin, a division of Penguin Putnam.

"The Triumph of Charlotte Salomon": Painter Charlotte Salomon, born in Berlin in 1917, died in Birkenau in 1943. I am grateful to Mary Felstiner for her brilliant biography and social history—*To Paint Her Life: Charlotte Salomon in the Nazi Era* (Berkeley: University of California Press, 1997)—which aided me in the writing of this poem.

Acknowledgments

I thank the editors of the following publications in which these poems, some in different versions, first appeared. *The American Poetry Review:* "Against Silence," "Angels of the Lower East Side," "Dog-God," "The Grief of Trees," "Late Words for My Sister," "Life Forms," "The Liz Christy–Bowery Houston Garden," "Mid-Life," "Midnight at the Third Street Sculpture Garden," "Monarchs of Parque Tranquilidad," "Sad Sestina," "Sisters in Perpetual Motion," "Solstice Bay," "Sonnet to the Imagination," "Why We Fear the Amish"; *The American Voice:* "Dylan's Fault"; *The Gettysburg Review:* "Elegy for a Secular Man"; *Heart Quarterly:* "The Abandoned Meander"; *Ploughshares:* "Raccoon"; *Prairie Schooner:* "In the Days of Awe"; *River Styx:* "Wants"; *Slate:* "Yoga"; *SOLO:* "Phaeton."

"Elegy for a Secular Man" first appeared in *The Gettysburg Review* 11, no. 2, and is reprinted here by permission of the editors.

"Raccoon" originally appeared in *Ploughshares* 23, no. 4.

"Yoga," copyright © 1996 by *Slate Magazine* (www.slate.com) and reprinted by permission.

For *"In The Days of Awe,"* I won the 1997 Virginia Faulkner Prize for Excellence in Writing from *Prairie Schooner* magazine.

I thank the Mary Bunting Institute of Radcliffe College for a 1995–1996 fellowship, during which I drafted many of these poems. An appointment as Visiting Scholar at the Center for Lesbian and Gay Studies at the City University of New York in 1998–1999 provided a supportive community in which to write. For research assistance on Charlotte Salomon, I thank the staff of the Joods Historisch Museum in Amsterdam; for travel funding, I gratefully acknowledge the Research and Graduate Study Office and the Department of English of the Pennsylvania State University. For artist residencies, I thank the MacDowell Colony and the Helene Wurlitzer Foundation of New

Mexico. I thank my parents for their love and understanding. Thanks to Phyllis and Si Hotch for the casita on the mesa and to Leslie Lawrence and Miriam Goodman for sharing the mowing. For assistance with this manuscript, I thank Rhonda Copelon, Miriam Goodman, Charlotte Holmes, Susanna Kaysen, Maxine Kumin, Leslie Lawrence, and Carolyn Sachs. I am grateful for the continuing interest and support of my colleagues in the English Department at the Pennsylvania State University.

Robin Becker, associate professor of English and Women's Studies at the Pennsylvania State University, is the author of four previous collections of poetry, *All-American Girl,* winner of the 1996 Lambda Literary Award for Lesbian Poetry; *Giacometti's Dog; Backtalk;* and *Personal Effects.* For an essay and long poem, she won the 1997 Virginia Faulkner Prize for Excellence in Writing from *Prairie Schooner* magazine. Becker has received fellowships from the Mary Bunting Institute of Radcliffe College, the Massachusetts Artists Foundation, and the National Endowment for the Arts. Her poems and book reviews have appeared in publications including *American Poetry Review, Boston Globe, Gettysburg Review,* and *Ploughshares.* Becker also serves as Poetry Editor for the *Women's Review of Books.* During the 1998–1999 academic year, she was a visiting scholar at the Center for Lesbian and Gay Studies at the City University of New York.